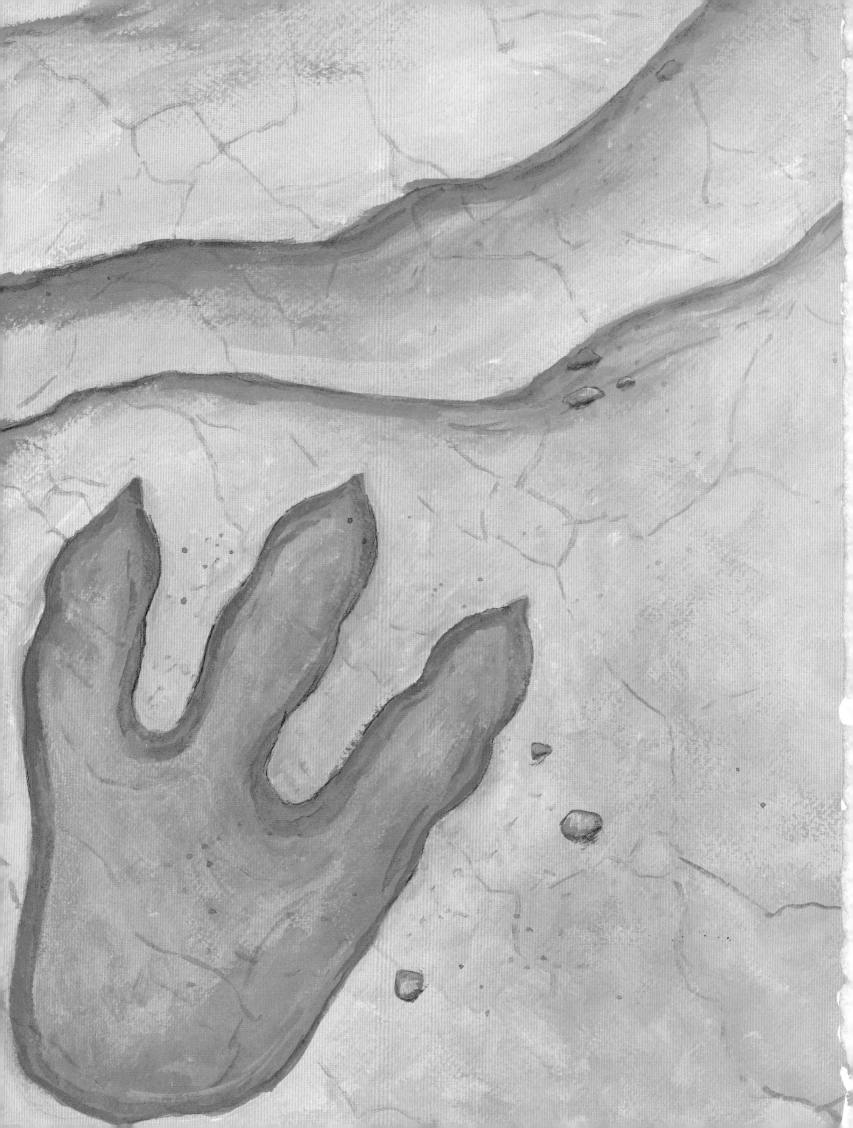

BARNUM BROWN
Dinosaur Hunter

DAVID SHELDON

Walker & Company

New York

On February 12, 1873, William and Clara Brown wanted to give their newborn son a special first name. Inspired by the famous showman P. T. Barnum, whose traveling circus happened to be in their town, Carbondale, Kansas, the Browns named their son Barnum. And true to his name, Barnum grew up to be an exceptional young man.

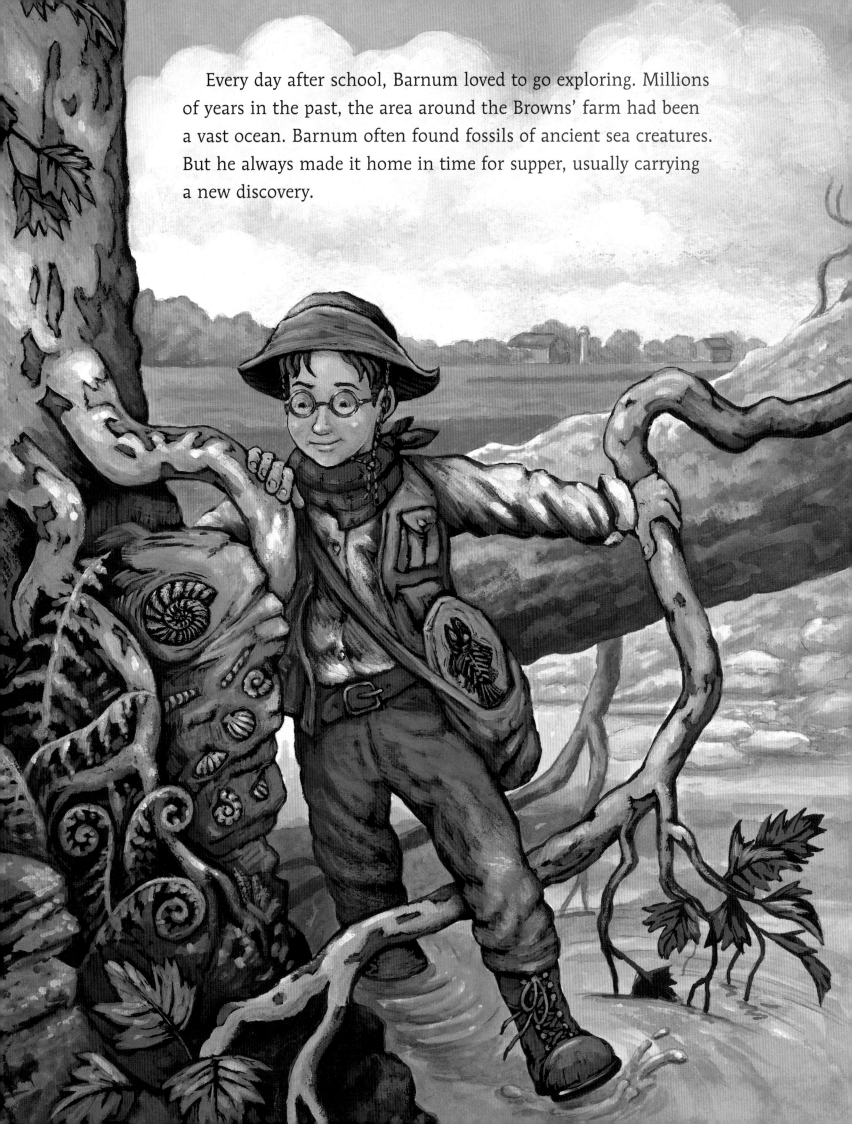

Every day after school, Barnum loved to go exploring. Millions of years in the past, the area around the Browns' farm had been a vast ocean. Barnum often found fossils of ancient sea creatures. But he always made it home in time for supper, usually carrying a new discovery.

After supper, the Browns would read the newspaper accounts of amazing new discoveries. The Great Dinosaur Rush of 1877 began when two dinosaur hunters, Edward Cope and Othniel Marsh, began a fierce rivalry, competing for dinosaur fossils in the American West. As a result, the lost world of dinosaurs was revealed like never before.

Barnum imagined what it might be like to explore for a seventy-foot-long *Apatosaurus*, come upon an armor plated *Stegosaurus*, or even be chased by a three-horned *Triceratops*! He just knew there had to be more amazing dinosaurs out there to discover.

Barnum's love of dinosaurs and exploring never left him. He went on to study dinosaurs (a subject called paleontology). Before long, he knew exactly what he wanted to do. He went to work for Henry F. Osborn, the director of the American Museum of Natural History, in New York City. The museum had bears, elk, sea turtles, herons, alligators, and countless other animal specimens and skeletons on display, but not one dinosaur. It would be Barnum's job to search for dinosaur fossils.

The best place to look for dinosaur fossils at the time was in the dry, forbidding "badlands" of the western United States and Canada. Beneath the clay and sandstone hills was a buried treasure of ancient animal bones. And that's where Barnum started searching.

In those days, before the automobile, the only way to get to a possible dinosaur site was by horse and wagon. The work could be hot, exhausting, and dangerous, but Barnum was determined to find something never seen before.

Before long, the American Museum of Natural History was receiving the extraordinary finds of Barnum Brown. Giant bones, protected in a burlap and plaster wrap (a method Barnum developed himself), arrived by the crateload.

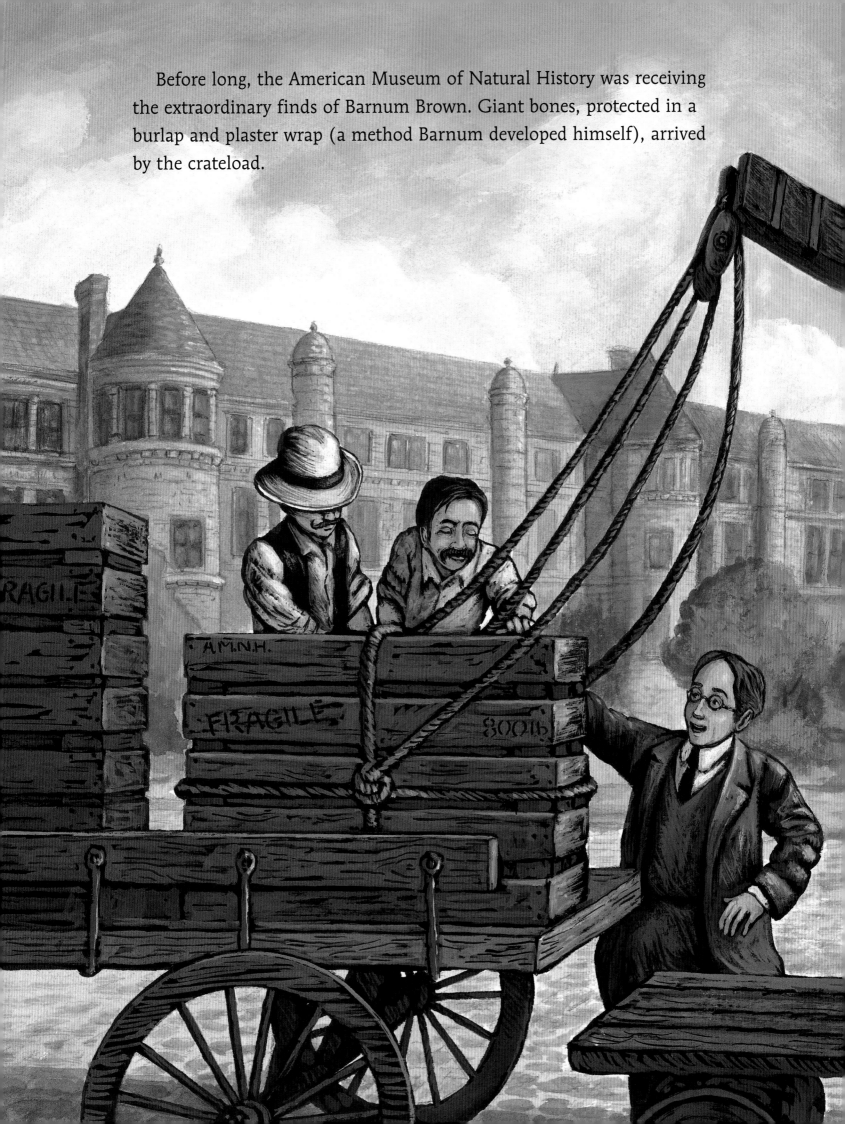

It was Henry Osborn's job to put together, describe, and name the new dinosaur discoveries. Other museums, such as the Carnegie Museum in Pittsburgh, had teams out searching for their own dinosaur fossils. Osborn dreamed about having the best collection of dinosaurs in the world, and he was counting on Barnum to help him realize his dream.

Barnum became so good at finding dinosaur fossils that Osborn would say he could smell the bones! Like his famous namesake, Barnum could be a real showman. Very often, he was found working merrily in a dusty dinosaur "quarry," carefully removing layers of clay and sandstone around a fossil while wearing a stylish hat, tie, and fur coat!

In 1898, Barnum's team of diggers began to uncover the first complete dinosaurs for the museum in Como Bluff, Wyoming, including an "old friend,"a huge *Apatosaurus*. As he worked, Barnum imagined what a family of *Apatosaurs* might have looked like.

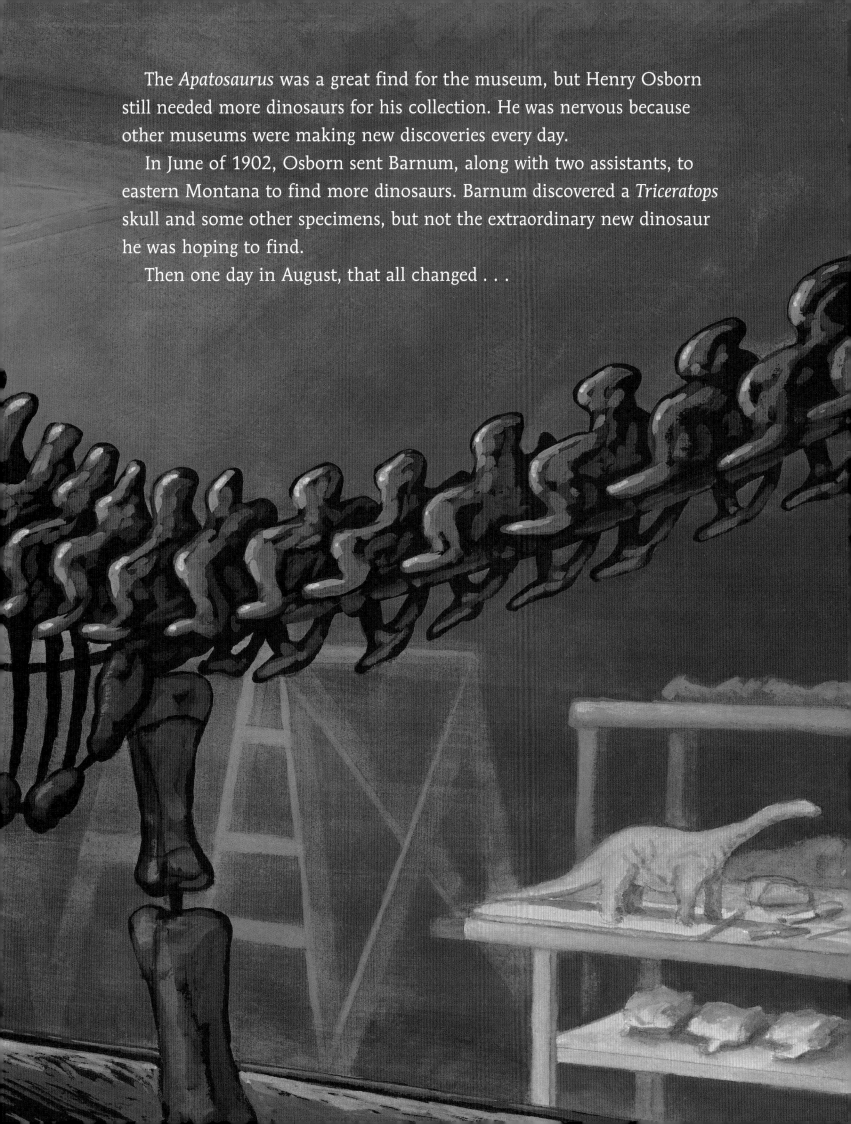

The *Apatosaurus* was a great find for the museum, but Henry Osborn still needed more dinosaurs for his collection. He was nervous because other museums were making new discoveries every day.

In June of 1902, Osborn sent Barnum, along with two assistants, to eastern Montana to find more dinosaurs. Barnum discovered a *Triceratops* skull and some other specimens, but not the extraordinary new dinosaur he was hoping to find.

Then one day in August, that all changed . . .

Barnum Brown was hot. As he wiped the sweat from his forehead, it awed him to think that this same sun may have shined down on some enormous dinosaur, millions of years in the past, whose bones were just waiting to be uncovered.

It had been a long day. Barnum was just about to give up looking any further, when something caught his eye.

Barnum knelt down and began to scrape away at the hard sandstone. Slowly, the telltale signs of a fossil began to emerge. Barnum's eyes widened. This was something he had never seen before. He called over his assistants, and together they set about the slow task of exposing the whole fossil.

Barnum was thrilled. Not only was this dinosaur a new discovery, but by the size of its teeth, it must have been a ferocious predator, the likes of which the modern world had never seen! It took two years to uncover all the pieces of this mystery dinosaur.

Back at the museum, Osborn and his staff assembled the pieces and were amazed by what they saw. Osborn named the new dinosaur *Tyrannosaurus Rex*, "Tyrant Lizard King." It had lived on the earth some sixty-five million years ago, surely spreading fear wherever it had roamed. Barnum discovered a second *T. Rex* in 1908, this one a nearly complete specimen.

When the final display was presented to the public, there were gasps throughout the hall. *T. Rex* was an overnight sensation, and Barnum Brown became known as the greatest of all dinosaur hunters!

Just two years after the discovery of the second *T. Rex*, Osborn sent Barnum to search the Red Deer River in the badlands of western Canada. Barnum designed a special flatboat to help his team explore the steep cliff walls for dinosaurs.

Not to be outdone in their own backyard, the Canadian government hired noted dinosaur hunter Charles H. Sternberg and his sons, George, Levi, and Charles Jr., to compete directly with Barnum's team. They constructed their own boat—and a new Dinosaur Rush was on!

The Sternbergs worked all day at their sites. It was difficult work, but the thrill of a new discovery kept them going. Just knowing Barnum Brown's team was digging nearby made them work even harder. The two groups enjoyed a friendly rivalry. But no one had a nose for finding dinosaurs like Barnum Brown.

Back at his quarry, Barnum and his team had another amazing find: *Saurolophus*. Emerging from the clay and sandstone were the fossilized remains of a creature that had not seen the light of day for seventy-five million years!

Because of their hard work and fierce competition, Barnum and the Sternbergs uncovered many important dinosaur fossils, including . . .

Saurolophus (saw-ROL-oh-fus)
Discovered by Brown's team, 1911.

Albertosaurus (el-ber-toh-SAWR-us)
First complete specimen discovered by
Brown's team, 1914.

Corythosaurus (co-RITH-oh-SAWR-us)
Discovered by Brown's team, 1912.

Styracosaurus (sty-RAK-o-SAWR-us)
Discovered by Brown's team, 1915.

Edmontonia (ed-mon-TO-ne-ah)
Discovered by the Sternbergs, 1917.

Hailed as the Second Great Dinosaur Rush, Barnum Brown's competition with the Sternbergs helped create one of the world's richest collections of dinosaurs. Osborn's dream had become a reality. Barnum Brown worked for the American Museum of Natural History for sixty-six years, eventually becoming Head Curator of Paleontology. After he retired, Barnum continued to give tours of his beloved dinosaurs, affectionately calling them his "children."

Digging Further into the Story

The first mounted dinosaur fossil put on display in the United States was a standing *Hadrosaur* skeleton constructed by Waterhouse Hawkins in 1868 for the Academy of Natural Sciences in Philadelphia. The public response was so overwhelming that a great rush began to find new dinosaur fossils.

Edward Cope, a paleontologist working for the academy, set out to find new dinosaurs in the American West. At the same time, Othniel Marsh from the Yale Peabody Museum put together his own team of dinosaur hunters and began searching the same area. At first, the two men were friendly, but as the competition for fossils became more intense, their friendship disintegrated. Both men sent teams (sometimes armed) to muscle out the other from new dinosaur sites. And when either man was finished with a site, he would have his men destroy any remaining fossils to keep them from his rival. Their feud even went on in the newspapers and scientific journals. Marsh publicly humiliated Cope by pointing out that Cope had mistakenly placed the head of a *Plesiosaur* on its tail rather than its neck! Yet their research helped establish western America as a prime dinosaur fossil location.

By the end of the nineteenth century, when Barnum Brown began his search, the study of dinosaurs had become an established and respected science. Barnum first discovered the lower jawbone and neck bones of *Tyrannosaurus Rex* (*T. Rex*) on an expedition in 1900, while searching for a *Triceratops* skull. Still searching for *Triceratops* fossils in 1902, he discovered the first nearly complete *T. Rex* skeleton along the steep bluffs of Hell Creek in eastern Montana. Returning to the same area in 1908, Barnum spied some vertebrae along a cliff wall that turned out to be one of the most complete *T. Rex* skeletons ever found. The original museum display aimed to have both *T. Rex* specimens included in a dramatic fighting scene. In the end, only one could be displayed because the museum simply didn't have enough room for both!

The original display of *T. Rex* had it standing upright with its tail dragging along on the ground. But further scientific research over the years revealed dinosaurs walked more like birds with their tails in the air to counterbalance all the weight up front. Barnum's *T. Rex* and the *Apatosaurus* were remounted in 1998 to show this new understanding.

After discovering *Tyrannosaurus Rex* (1902), Barnum discovered many new dinosaurs and, with the permission of the museum, named many as well, including *Ankylosaurus* (1908), *Kritosaurus* (1910), *Saurolophus* (1911), *Hypacrosaurus* (1913), *Corythosaurus* (1914), *Anchiceratops* (1914), *Leptoceratops* (1914), *Prosaurolophus* (1916), *Dromaeosaurus* (1922), and *Pachycephalosaurus* (1943).

Barnum worked for the American Museum of Natural History as scientist and curator for sixty-six years. If you visit the museum, be sure to look for his name under the many dinosaurs on display there, including *Tyrannosaurus Rex*.

*The following museums contain the actual dinosaur fossils
from this story:*

American Museum of Natural History
79th Street and Central Park West
New York, New York 10025
Tel: 212-313-7278 Web site: www.amnh.org

Carnegie Museum of Natural History
4400 Forbes Avenue
Pittsburgh, Pennsylvania 15213
Tel: 412-622-3131 Web site: www.carnegiemnh.org

Royal Tyrrell Museum
Highway 838 Midland Provincial Park
Drumheller, Alberta, Canada T0J 0Y0
Tel: 888-440-4240 Web site: www.tyrrellmuseum.com

The Academy of Natural Sciences of Philadelphia
1900 Ben Franklin Parkway
Philadelphia, Pennsylvania 19103
Tel: 215-299-1000 Web site: www.acnatsci.org

Yale Peabody Museum
170 Whitney Avenue
New Haven, Connecticut 06511
Tel: 203-432-5050 Web site: www.peabody.yale.edu

Royal Ontario Museum
100 Queen's Park
Toronto, Ontario, Canada ON M5S 2C6
Tel: 416-516-8000 Web site: www.rom.on.ca

Resource Guide *(Books for young readers are marked with an asterisk)*

American Museum of Natural History, 125 Years of Expedition and Discovery, Lyle Rexer and
    Rachel Klein, Harry N. Abrams Publishers in association with the AMNH, 1995.

Bones for Barnum Brown: Adventures of a Dinosaur Hunter, Roland T. Bird, Texas Christian
    University Press, 1985.

Field Guide to Dinosaurs: The Essential Handbook for Travelers in the Mesozoic, Henry Gee and
    Luis V. Rey, Barron's, 2003.

"Field Reports and Barnum Brown's Field Notebooks," The American Museum of Natural History,
    Web site: www.amnh.org.

* *Tyrannosaurus Rex and Barnum Brown,* Brooke Hartzog, Rosen Publishing Group, 1999.

* *The Ultimate Dinosaur Book,* David Lambert, DK Publishing Inc., 1993.

* *What Color Is That Dinosaur?,* Lowell Dingus, Millbrook Press, 1994.

* *The World of Dinosaurs,* Michael Benton, Kingfisher, 2004.

For my parents, Roger and Lois Sheldon,
who always encouraged me to get out there
and explore. —D. S.

First published in the United States of America in 2006 by Walker Publishing Company, Inc.
Distributed to the trade by Holtzbrinck Publishers
For information about permission to reproduce selections from
this book, write to Permissions, Walker & Company,
104 Fifth Avenue, New York, New York 10011

Library of Congress Cataloging-in-Publication Data
Sheldon, David.
Barnum Brown : dinosaur hunter / David Sheldon.
p.   cm.
ISBN-10: 0-8027-9602-8 • ISBN-13: 978-0-8027-9602-8 (hardcover)
ISBN-10: 0-8027-9603-6 • ISBN-13: 978-0-8027-9603-5 (reinforced)
1. Brown, Barnum—Juvenile literature. 2. Paleontologists—United States—
Biography—Juvenile literature. 3. Dinosaurs—Juvenile literature. I. Title.
QE707.B77S54 2006   560.92—dc22   2006000471

The illustrations for this book were created with India ink, gouache,
and acrylic paint on 140-lb. coldpress watercolor paper.
Book design by Donna Mark
Visit Walker & Company's Web site at www.walkeryoungreaders.com
Printed in China

10 9 8 7 6 5 4 3 2 1

All papers used by Walker & Company are natural, recyclable products made
from wood grown in well-managed forests. The manufacturing processes
conform to the environmental regulations of the country of origin.

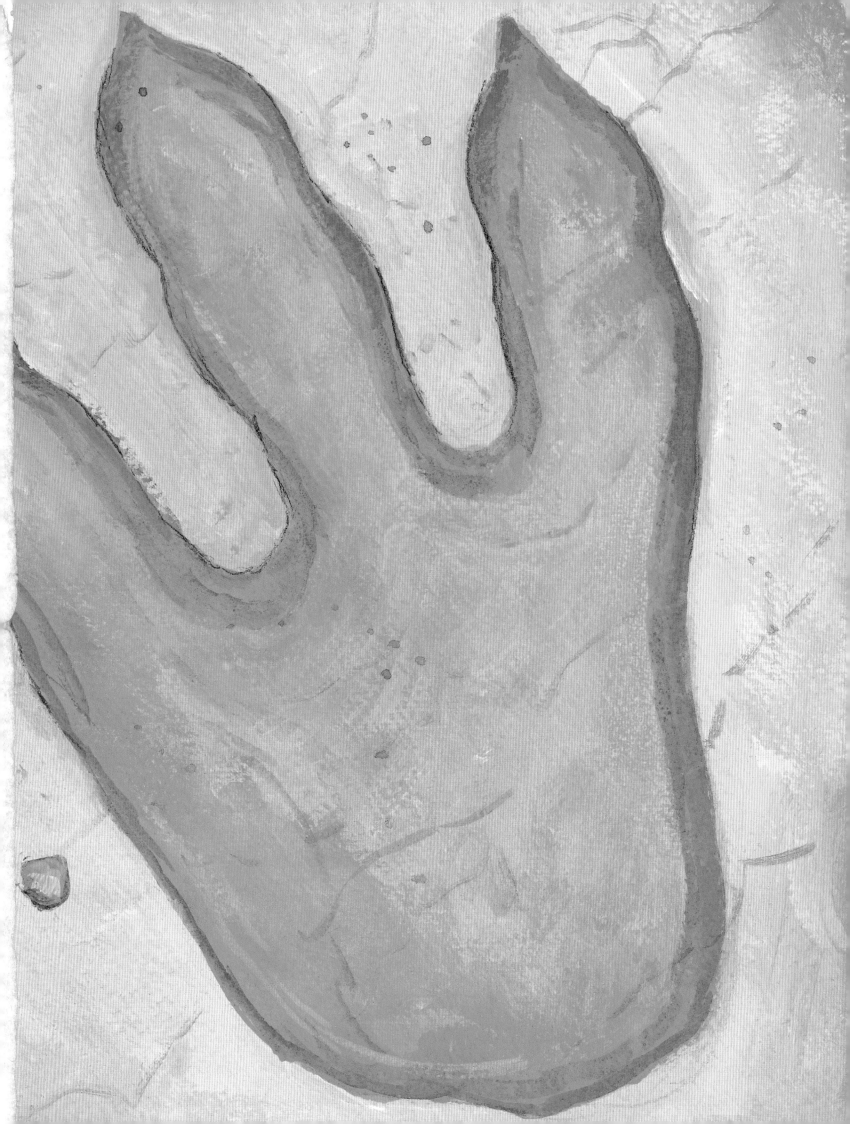